MIDDLE
eastern

MIDDLE eastern

AROMATIC DISHES FROM A VARIED CUISINE

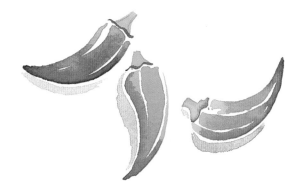

introduction by

soheila kimberley

southwater

This edition is published by Southwater

Southwater is an imprint of Anness Publishing Ltd
Hermes House, 88–89 Blackfriars Road, London SE1 8HA
tel. 020 7401 2077; fax 020 7633 9499
www.southwaterbooks.com; info@anness.com

UK agent: The Manning Partnership Ltd, tel. 01225 478444; fax 01225 478440;
sales@manning-partnership.co.uk
UK distributor: Grantham Book Services Ltd, tel. 01476 541080; fax 01476 541061;
orders@gbs.tbs-ltd.co.uk
North American agent/distributor: National Book Network, tel. 301 459 3366; fax 301 429 5746; www.nbnbooks.com
Australian agent/distributor: Pan Macmillan Australia, tel. 1300 135 113; fax 1300 135 103;
customer.service@macmillan.com.au
New Zealand agent/distributor: David Bateman Ltd, tel. (09) 415 7664; fax (09) 415 8892

Publisher Joanna Lorenz
Senior Cookery Editor Linda Fraser
Project Editor Zoe Antoniou
Designer Ian Sandom
Illustrations Madeleine David
Recipes Jacqueline Clark, Roz Denny, Nicola Diggins, Matthew Drennan, Joanna Farrow,
Sarah Gates, Judy Jackson, Soheila Kimberley, Sue Maggs, Annie Nichols, Jenny Stacey, Liz Trigg
and Steven Wheeler
Cover: *Photography* Nicki Dowey *Stylist* Emma Patmore *Design* Wilson Harvey

Previously published as part of the Classic cookery series

Typeset by MC Typeset Ltd, Rochester, Kent

1 3 5 7 9 10 8 6 4 2

For all recipes, quantities are given in both metric and imperial measures, and, where appropriate, measures are also
given in standard cups and spoons. Follow one set, but not a mixture, because they are not interchangeable.

Picture on frontispiece shows (clockwise from top left):
Koftas in Tomato Sauce, Lamb Couscous and Lamb Kebabs.

CONTENTS

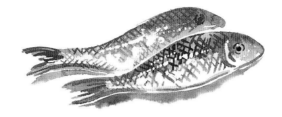

INTRODUCTION

For over three thousand years the Middle East has been the crucible of many civilizations – the Babylonian, Armenian, Assyrian, Persian, Greek and Roman to name just six – and in the process it has acquired a rich and cosmopolitan character.

While most of us eat to live, the typical Middle East dweller lives to eat. There is, however, more to it than that and food plays a very important social role. An old Persian saying sums up the attitude to food perfectly: *Mehman Hediyah Khodust* (A guest is God's gift). And, indeed, there is no better way to look after a guest than to give him or her good food.

While many Middle Eastern dishes have similar origins, every region, every country, every town and, in days gone by, every family, had their own recipes and their own ways of preparing a universal dish. As a result, many dishes have historical

significance. The Persian *khoresh*, for example, is made up of a balance of ingredients that reflects the ancient Parthians' belief in the eternal battle between light and darkness. This balance continues to be the basis of Persian cuisine, although many cooks may be unaware of its origins. Today, many of these dishes have intermingled between various countries so that the area has developed a wide range of dishes to suit all tastes.

Rice, which was once a luxury ingredient grown along the northern borders of Persia around the Caspian Sea, is now one of the staples of Middle Eastern cuisine. Originally the diet consisted mainly of millet porridge, coarse bread, olives, figs, beans, cheese and milk.

Important ingredients nowadays include milk, honey, yogurt, cheese, fruit and vegetables, especially garlic and onions. Olive oil has long been recognized throughout the Middle East for its healthy properties. Meat and poultry are valued for their protein content, and if meat is not used, dried beans and other pulses are substituted.

Puddings and desserts are not common in the Middle East. The main courses tend to be very filling so fruit is generally the preferred choice at the end of a meal. Sweetmeats are served on festive occasions, or when entertaining guests for tea.

There are so many traditional recipes to experiment with that the art of cooking becomes an integral part of the enjoyment of food. Discover the essence of the Middle East and introduce this exciting cuisine to your friends and family.

Picture on right (clockwise from top): Fattoush, Lentil Soup and Hummus.

INGREDIENTS

A walk through a bazaar in the Middle East provides the best introduction to local ingredients. Shop after shop is packed with aromatics and spices, from rose petals to cinnamon and saffron. You can buy any combination you choose, but the popular herbs and spices are chives, cinnamon, paprika, saffron and turmeric.

AUBERGINE There are countless ways of preparing this vegetable, but the secret of preserving the delicate flavour lies in first removing any bitterness. This is done by slicing or dicing the aubergine into a colander, sprinkling it with salt and allowing it to drain. It is rinsed and dried before use.

BROAD BEANS Broad beans are available frozen from any supermarket or fresh when in season. Only the tender green centre of the bean is

used in Middle Eastern cooking so they need to be peeled if they are frozen or podded and peeled if bought fresh.

CINNAMON It is the powdered form of this spice that is widely used in all sorts of Middle

A selection of spices (left to right from top row): ground sumac, saffron threads, paprika, cinnamon sticks, turmeric, cardamom pods, ground nutmeg, whole nutmegs and cumin seeds.

Eastern recipes. It is invariably used in different types of *khoresh*.

CUMIN The delicate aroma of this spice is a perfect complement to many vegetable dishes and salads. Cumin seeds have a flavour similar to that of caraway. In Middle Eastern cooking, cumin is used either whole or ground.

DRIED LIMES *Limu amani* are available from Middle Eastern or Greek shops, either whole or crushed, and they make a very good alternative to lemon. They are usually cooked with meat and fresh herbs.

GARLIC Used extensively throughout the Middle East, garlic is valued for its health-giving properties as well as its flavour.

HERBS Chives, coriander, dill, marjoram, mint and parsley are among the most important ingredients in any Middle Eastern kitchen. They are served fresh, traditionally on a separate plate, to accompany the main dishes. Fresh herbs are often offered with cheese, cooked with meat and rice, mixed into salads and used in stuffings for vegetables. Chopped herbs are used in handfuls, rather than spoonfuls, in all sorts of cooked dishes.

NUTMEG Nutmegs are the hard aromatic seeds that come from an evergreen tree. The spice is used extensively all over the world. Whole nutmegs can be grated for cooking, but Middle Eastern dishes usually use the ground spice.

NUTS Nuts are widely used in Middle Eastern cooking and are often combined with rice, but how they are used depends on the country. In Iran, for instance, walnuts are ground, cooked with either chicken or duck and made into a delicious sauce with pomegranate juice or sour cherries. Almonds, hazelnuts, pistachio nuts and pine nuts are not only combined with rice and used in savoury stuffings, but they are also used to fill sweetmeats, such as baklava.

PAPRIKA Although paprika is often associated with Eastern Europe, it is widely used in the Middle East in soups, meat dishes, various salad dressings and garnishes.

RED PEPPERS Widely used, red peppers make a delicious meal when stuffed or cooked with meat and aubergines. When grilled, they acquire a smoky flavour, and are a tasty salad ingredient.

RICE Rice is the most common ingredient in Middle Eastern cooking. Basmati rice has an exquisite taste and aroma. Long grain American rice gives good results, while short grain rice is often used for puddings. The smell and flavour of Iranian rice is particularly interesting.

SAFFRON Derived from the dried stamens of a type of crocus, saffron has a superb aroma and flavour. It also adds a delicate colour to food. For the best results, it should be ground to a powder and diluted in a small amount of boiling water before using.

SPINACH Fresh baby spinach leaves are available from greengrocers and supermarkets throughout the year. In the Middle East, spinach is often cooked with meat or combined with yogurt to make a popular vegetarian starter.

SUMAC These edible red berries are dried and crushed to a powder and are delicious sprinkled on kebabs, fish dishes and salads.

TURMERIC This spice originated in Iran. It adds a distinctive flavour and rich yellow colour to meat and rice dishes. It is widely used throughout the Middle East.

VINE LEAVES When stuffed with meat, lentils and herbs, these make delicious starters.

ZERESHK This is a small sour berry that grows on trees by the water in the warmer part of Iran. It is traditionally served with a number of Persian rice dishes.

A selection of ingredients (clockwise from board): dried limes, zereshk, long grain rice, basmati and short grain rice.

SPINACH AND LEMON SOUP WITH MEATBALLS

This dish, *Aarshe Saak*, is almost standard fare in many parts of the Middle East. Add the lemon juice gradually, according to your taste.

INGREDIENTS
2 large onions
45ml/3 tbsp oil
15ml/1 tbsp ground turmeric
90g/3¹/₂oz/¹/₂ cup yellow split peas
225g/8oz/2 cups minced lamb
450g/1lb spinach, chopped
50g/2oz/¹/₂ cup rice flour
juice of 2 lemons
4 eggs, beaten
salt and freshly ground black pepper
1–2 garlic cloves, very finely chopped and
30ml/2 tbsp chopped fresh mint,
to garnish

SERVES 6

1 Chop one onion. Heat 30ml/2 tbsp of the oil in a large frying pan and fry the onion until golden. Add the turmeric, split peas and 1.2 litres/2 pints/5 cups water and bring to the boil. Reduce the heat and simmer for about 20 minutes.

2 Grate the other onion. Put it into a mixing bowl, add the minced lamb and seasoning and mix well. Using your hands, form the mixture into small meatballs, about the size of walnuts. Carefully add to the saucepan and simmer for 10 minutes, then add the chopped spinach, cover and simmer for 20 minutes.

3 Mix the flour with 250ml/8fl oz/1 cup cold water to make a smooth paste, then slowly add it to the saucepan, stirring all the time to prevent lumps forming. Stir in the lemon juice, season with salt and pepper and cook over a gentle heat for 20 minutes.

4 Heat the remaining oil in a small pan and fry the garlic briefly until golden. Stir in the mint and remove the pan from the heat. Remove the soup from the heat and stir in the beaten eggs. Sprinkle the garlic and mint garnish over the soup and serve.

LENTIL SOUP

This traditional Turkish soup makes an ideal winter starter, or serve it with chunks of crusty bread and butter for a wholesome lunch.

INGREDIENTS
45ml/3 tbsp olive oil
1 large onion, chopped
1 celery stick, chopped
400g/14oz/2½ cups red lentils
1.2 litres/2 pints/5 cups meat stock
4–5 tomatoes
juice of 1 lemon
2.5ml/½ tsp chilli powder (optional)
salt and freshly ground black pepper
celery leaf, to garnish

SERVES 4

COOK'S TIP
Yellow and/or brown lentils can be used instead of red lentils, if you prefer. They may require slightly longer to cook.

1 Heat the oil in a large saucepan and cook the onion and celery over a gentle heat, until soft. Add the lentils and stock to the pan, bring to the boil and then simmer for 25 minutes, or until the lentils are soft.

2 Peel the tomatoes by dipping them into boiling water for about 30 seconds to loosen the skins.

3 Roughly chop the tomatoes and add them to the saucepan with the lemon juice, salt and pepper and the chilli powder, if using. Simmer for a further 10 minutes and serve garnished with a celery leaf.

BÖREKS

In Turkey, little stuffed pastries are very popular. They are easy to make and are ideal for starters, snacks or finger canapés.

INGREDIENTS
225g/8oz feta cheese, grated
225g/8oz mozzarella cheese, grated
2 eggs, beaten
45ml/3 tbsp chopped fresh parsley
45ml/3 tbsp snipped fresh chives
45ml/3tbsp chopped fresh mint
pinch of nutmeg
225g/8oz filo pastry
45–60ml/3–4 tbsp melted butter
freshly ground black pepper

MAKES 35–40

1 Preheat the oven to 180°C/350°F/Gas 4. In a bowl, blend the feta and mozzarella cheeses with the beaten eggs. Add the chopped herbs, season with black pepper and nutmeg, and stir well to mix.

2 Cut the sheets of pastry into four rectangular strips approximately 7.5cm/3in wide. Cover all but one or two strips of the pastry with a damp cloth to prevent them from drying out.

3 Brush one strip of pastry at a time with a little melted butter.

4 Place 5ml/1 tsp of filling at the bottom edge. Fold one corner over the filling to make a triangle shape. Continue folding the pastry over itself until you get to the end of the strip. Keep making triangles until all the mixture is used up.

5 Place the *Böreks* on a greased baking tray and bake in the oven for about 30 minutes until golden brown and crisp. Serve warm or cold.

COOK'S TIP
A mixture of almost any cheese can be used but avoid using cream cheese. The Greek version of these is stuffed with spinach and feta. You could try this as an alternative, if you like, adding cooked spinach (stalks removed) in place of herbs and mozzarella cheese.

BAKED EGGS WITH HERBS AND VEGETABLES

Eggs, baked or fried as omelettes with vegetables, herbs or even meat, are very popular.

INGREDIENTS

2–3 saffron strands
8 eggs
2 leeks
115g/4oz fresh spinach
½ iceberg lettuce
4 spring onions
45ml/3 tbsp chopped fresh parsley
45ml/3 tbsp snipped fresh chives
45ml/3 tbsp chopped fresh coriander
1 garlic clove, crushed
30ml/2 tbsp chopped walnuts (optional)
25g/1oz/2 tbsp butter
salt and freshly ground black pepper
yogurt and pitta bread, to
serve (optional)

SERVES 4–6

1 Preheat the oven to 180°C/350°F/Gas 4. Soak the saffron strands in 15ml/1 tbsp boiling water.

2 Beat the eggs in a large bowl. Chop the leeks, spinach, lettuce and spring onions very finely.

3 Add the chopped vegetables to the eggs, together with the herbs, garlic, and walnuts, if using. Season with salt and pepper, add the saffron water and stir well.

4 Melt the butter in a large ovenproof dish. Pour in the vegetable and egg mixture.

5 Bake in the oven for 35–40 minutes until the egg mixture is set and the top is golden. Serve hot or cold, cut into wedges, with yogurt and pitta bread, if liked.

COOK'S TIP
To bring out their flavour, lightly toast the walnuts in a moderate oven, or under a hot grill before chopping.

HUMMUS WITH PAN-FRIED COURGETTES

Pan-fried courgettes are perfect for dipping into home-made hummus. You can also use them to stuff pitta breads, together with falafel. Tahini, or sesame seed paste, is available from Jewish or Arabic delicatessens. It is worth making twice the quantity as hummus freezes well.

INGREDIENTS
225g/8oz can chick-peas
2 garlic cloves, roughly chopped
90ml/6 tbsp lemon juice
60ml/4 tbsp tahini paste
75ml/5 tbsp olive oil, plus extra to serve
5ml/1 tsp ground cumin
450g/1lb small courgettes
salt and freshly ground black pepper
paprika, pitta bread and black olives,
to serve

SERVES 4

1 Drain the chick-peas, reserving the liquid from the can, and tip them into a food processor or blender. Process to a smooth purée, adding a small amount of the reserved liquid, if necessary.

2 Mix the garlic, lemon juice and tahini paste together and add to the food processor or blender. Process until smooth. With the machine running, gradually add 45ml/3 tbsp of the olive oil through the feeder tube or lid.

3 Add the ground cumin, with salt and pepper to taste. Process to mix, then scrape the hummus into a bowl. Cover and chill until required.

4 Top and tail the courgettes. Slice them lengthways into even-size pieces.

5 Heat the remaining oil in a large frying pan. Season the courgettes and fry for 2–3 minutes on each side, until just tender.

6 Divide the courgettes among four plates. Spoon a portion of hummus on to each plate, sprinkle with paprika, add two or three slices of pitta bread and serve with olives.

COOK'S TIP
Hummus is also delicious served with pan-fried or grilled aubergine slices.

DOLMEH

These dainty vine-leaf parcels are very popular in Mediterranean countries too. Traditionally, they are served as part of a Greek *mezze*.

INGREDIENTS
15ml/1 tbsp olive oil
115g/4oz/1 cup minced beef
30ml/2 tbsp pine nuts
1 onion, chopped
15ml/1 tbsp chopped fresh coriander
5ml/1 tsp ground cumin
15ml/1 tbsp tomato purée
8 vine leaves
salt and freshly ground black pepper
green and red pepper salad, to serve

FOR THE TOMATO SAUCE
150ml/¼ pint/⅔ cup passata
150ml/¼ pint/⅔ cup beef stock
10ml/2 tsp caster sugar

SERVES 4

1 Heat the oil in a pan. Add the minced beef, pine nuts and onion. Cook for 5 minutes, until the meat is browned.

2 Stir in the fresh coriander, ground cumin and tomato purée. Cook for 3 minutes more and season well.

COOK'S TIP
If vine leaves are unavailable, use lettuce or cabbage leaves dropped in boiling water until wilted.

3 Preheat the oven to 180°C/350°F/Gas 4. Place eight vine leaves, shiny side down, on a work surface. Spoon some of the filling in the centre of each leaf and fold the stalk end over the filling. Roll up the parcel towards the tip of the leaf and place in a lightly greased flameproof casserole dish, seam side down.

4 To make the sauce, mix together the passata, stock and sugar and pour it over the Dolmeh. Cover and cook in the oven for about 30 minutes. Serve with green and red pepper salad.

YOGURT AND CUCUMBER DIP

This dish, *Tacik*, is similar to *Tzatziki*, a Greek cucumber salad dressed with yogurt, mint and garlic. It is typically served with grilled lamb or chicken, but it is also good with salmon or trout.

INGREDIENTS
1 cucumber
5ml/1 tsp salt
45ml/3 tbsp finely chopped fresh mint,
plus a few sprigs to garnish
1 garlic clove, crushed
5ml/1 tsp caster sugar
200ml/7fl oz/1 cup Greek-style yogurt
paprika, to garnish (optional)

SERVES 4

COOK'S TIP
If preparing this dish in a hurry, there is no need to salt the cucumber. It will have a crunchier texture and will be slightly less sweet.

1 Peel the cucumber. Reserve a little of it to use as a garnish, if you wish, and then cut the rest in half lengthways. Carefully remove all the seeds with a teaspoon and discard them.

2 Slice the peeled cucumber thinly and combine it with salt, then leave it for about 15–20 minutes. The salt softens the cucumber and draws out any bitter juices.

3 Combine the mint, garlic, sugar and yogurt in a bowl, reserving a few sprigs of mint to garnish.

4 Rinse the cucumber in a sieve under cold running water to flush away the salt. Drain well and combine with the yogurt. Garnish with the reserved cucumber and mint and serve cold. If liked, garnish the dish with paprika as well.

AUBERGINE DIP

ubergines are very popular in the Middle East and they are virtually a staple food in Israel.

INGREDIENTS
2 aubergines, about 275g/10oz each
2 onions, chopped
150ml/¹/₄ pint/²/₃ cup olive oil
3 garlic cloves, crushed
juice of 1 lemon
salt and freshly ground black pepper
sprigs of fresh coriander, to garnish
black and green olives, to serve

SERVES 4 AS A STARTER
OR MORE AS A DIP

1 Preheat the grill. Cut the aubergines in half lengthways and put them on a sheet of foil, skin side up. Grill at least 5cm/2in from the heat for 20 minutes. The skin will start to wrinkle and the flesh will become slightly smoky and soft.

2 Sauté the onions in about 60ml/4 tbsp of the oil. Add the garlic and cook until the mixture is soft but not brown. Season.

3 Scoop the flesh out of the aubergine halves and put it into a blender or food processor with the onion and garlic. Add the lemon juice.

4 With the blades running, slowly pour in the remaining olive oil to make a very smooth mixture. Taste again for seasoning.

5 Spoon the aubergine dip into a small serving bowl and garnish it with sprigs of fresh coriander. Serve cold with black and green olives.

FISH WITH RICE

his Arabic dish, *Sayadieh*, is very popular in the Lebanon. It makes a delicious and substantial meal.

INGREDIENTS
juice of 1 lemon
45ml/3 tbsp oil
900g/2lb cod steaks
4 large onions, chopped
5ml/1 tsp ground cumin
2–3 saffron strands
1 litre/1³/4 pints/4 cups fish stock
450g/1lb/2²/3 cups basmati, or other long grain rice
50g/2oz/¹/2 cup pine nuts, lightly toasted
salt and freshly ground black pepper
fresh parsley, to garnish

SERVES 4–6

COOK'S TIP
When cooking the rice take care that the saucepan does not boil dry. Check it occasionally and add more stock or water, if necessary.

1 Blend together the lemon juice and 15ml/1 tbsp of the oil in a shallow dish. Add the fish steaks, turning them to coat thoroughly, then cover and leave to marinate for 30 minutes.

2 Heat the remaining oil in a large saucepan or flameproof casserole and fry the onions for 5–6 minutes, until golden, stirring occasionally.

3 Drain the fish, reserving the marinade, and add to the pan. Fry for 1–2 minutes each side, until lightly golden, then add the ground cumin, saffron strands and a little salt and pepper.

4 Pour in the fish stock and the reserved marinade, bring to the boil and simmer very gently over a low heat for 5–10 minutes until the fish is nearly done.

5 Transfer the fish to a plate and add the rice to the stock. Bring to the boil, then reduce the heat and simmer very gently over a low heat for 15 minutes, until nearly all the stock has been absorbed.

6 Arrange the fish on the rice and cover. Steam the dish over a low heat for a further 15–20 minutes.

7 Transfer the fish to a plate, then spoon the rice on to a large flat dish and arrange the fish on top. Sprinkle with toasted pine nuts and garnish with parsley.

PRAWNS IN TOMATO SAUCE

Prawns are popular everywhere in the Middle East. This delicious recipe is an easy way of making the most of them.

INGREDIENTS
30ml/2 tbsp oil
2 onions, finely chopped
2–3 garlic cloves, crushed
5–6 tomatoes, peeled and chopped
30ml/2 tbsp tomato purée
120ml/4fl oz/1/2 cup fish stock or water
2.5ml/1/2 tsp ground cumin
2.5ml/1/2 tsp ground cinnamon
450g/1lb raw, peeled Mediterranean prawns
juice of 1 lemon
salt and freshly ground black pepper
fresh parsley, to garnish
rice, to serve

SERVES 4

1 Heat the oil in a large frying pan or saucepan and fry the onions for about 3–4 minutes, until golden. Add the garlic, fry for 1 minute, and then stir in the tomatoes.

2 Blend the tomato purée with the stock or water and stir into the pan with the cumin, cinnamon and seasoning. Simmer, covered, over a low heat for 15 minutes, stirring occasionally. Do not allow to boil.

3 Add the prawns and lemon juice and simmer the sauce for 10–15 minutes over a low to moderate heat until the prawns are cooked and the stock is reduced by about half.

4 Garnish the prawns with fresh parsley and serve them with plain boiled rice.

SWORDFISH KEBABS

Fish is particularly delicious when cooked over hot charcoal and this dish makes a wonderful alternative to meat kebabs.

INGREDIENTS
900g/2lb swordfish steaks
45ml/3 tbsp olive oil
juice of 1/2 lemon
1 garlic clove, crushed
5ml/1 tsp paprika
3 tomatoes, quartered
2 onions, cut into wedges
salt and freshly ground black pepper
salad, to serve

SERVES 4–6

COOK'S TIP
Almost any type of firm white fish can be used for this recipe.

1 Cut the swordfish into large cubes and place them in a dish.

2 Blend together the olive oil, lemon juice, garlic, paprika and salt and pepper in a small mixing bowl and pour this over the fish. Cover it loosely with clear film and leave it to marinate in a cool place for up to 2 hours.

3 Thread the fish cubes on to skewers, alternating them with pieces of tomato and onion.

4 Grill the swordfish kebabs over hot charcoal for 5–10 minutes, basting them frequently with the remaining marinade and turning them occasionally. Serve with plenty of fresh salad.

BAKED FISH WITH TAHINI SAUCE

This simple dish is a great favourite in many Arab countries, particularly Egypt, the Lebanon and Syria. Choose any whole white fish, such as sea bass, hake, bream or snapper.

INGREDIENTS
*1 whole fish, about 1.1kg/2¹/₂lb, scaled
and cleaned
10ml/2 tsp coriander seeds
4 garlic cloves, sliced
10ml/2 tsp harissa sauce
90ml/6 tbsp olive oil
6 plum tomatoes, sliced
1 mild onion, sliced
3 preserved lemons, or 1 fresh lemon
plenty of fresh herbs, such as bay leaves,
thyme and rosemary
salt and freshly ground black pepper
fresh herbs, to garnish*

FOR THE SAUCE
*75ml/3fl oz/²/₃ cup light tahini paste
juice of 1 lemon
1 garlic clove, crushed
45ml/3 tbsp finely chopped fresh parsley
or coriander*

SERVES 4

1 Preheat the oven to 200°C/400°F/Gas 6. Grease the base and sides of a large shallow ovenproof dish or a roasting tin.

2 Slash the fish diagonally on both sides with a sharp knife. Finely crush the coriander seeds and garlic with a pestle and mortar. Mix with the harissa sauce and about 60ml/4 tbsp of the olive oil.

3 Spread a little of the harissa paste inside the cavity of the fish. Spread the rest over each side of the fish and set aside.

COOK'S TIP
You can use small whole fish, such as red mullet, or even cod or haddock steaks, for this dish. Remember to reduce the cooking time slightly.

4 Scatter the tomato slices, onion and the preserved or fresh lemon into the dish. (Thinly slice the lemon if using a fresh one.) Sprinkle over the remaining oil and season well with salt and pepper. Lay the prepared fish on top and tuck plenty of fresh herbs around it.

5 Bake the dish in the preheated oven, uncovered, for about 25 minutes, or until the fish has turned opaque – you can test it by piercing the thickest part with a knife.

6 Meanwhile, make the sauce. Put the tahini paste, lemon juice, garlic and parsley or coriander in a small saucepan with 120ml/4fl oz/½ cup water and add a little salt and pepper to taste. Cook the sauce gently until it is smooth and heated through. Serve it in a separate dish, with the fish on a plate, garnished with herbs.

STUFFED SARDINES

This dish does not take a lot of preparation time and it is a meal in itself. Just serve it with a crisp green salad tossed in a fresh lemon vinaigrette to make it complete.

INGREDIENTS
900g/2lb fresh sardines
30ml/2 tbsp olive oil
75g/3oz/½ cup wholemeal breadcrumbs
50g/2oz/¼ cup sultanas
50g/2oz/½ cup pine nuts
50g/2oz canned anchovy fillets, drained
60ml/4 tbsp chopped fresh parsley
1 onion, finely chopped
salt and freshly ground black pepper

SERVES 4

1 Preheat the oven to 200°C/400°F/Gas 6. Gut the sardines and wipe them out thoroughly with kitchen paper. Heat about 15ml/1 tbsp of the oil in a frying pan and fry the breadcrumbs until golden brown.

2 Add the sultanas, pine nuts, drained anchovies, chopped parsley, onion and seasoning and mix well.

3 Carefully fill each of the cleaned sardines with the herb and breadcrumb stuffing. When the sardine is full, close it firmly together and place it in the bottom of an ovenproof dish.

4 As the sardines are stuffed, scatter a little of the remaining filling and drizzle a little of the remaining olive oil over them. Bake the fish for 30 minutes in the preheated oven, then serve at once.

MIDDLE EASTERN SEA BREAM

 Buy the smallest sea bream you can find to cook whole, allowing one for two people.

INGREDIENTS
*1.75kg/4lb whole sea bream, or 2 smaller
sea bream
30ml/2 tbsp olive oil
75g/3oz/³⁄₄ cup pine nuts
1 large onion, finely chopped
450g/1lb ripe tomatoes, roughly chopped
75g/3oz/¹⁄₂ cup raisins
1.5ml/¹⁄₄ tsp ground cinnamon
1.5ml/¹⁄₄ tsp ground mixed spice
45ml/3 tbsp chopped fresh mint
225g/8oz/1 cup long grain rice
3 lemon slices
300ml/¹⁄₂ pint/1¹⁄₄ cups fish stock
fresh mint sprigs, to garnish*

SERVES 4

VARIATION
If you can't find pine nuts, substitute the same quantity of blanched almonds, split in half before stir-frying.

---

1 Trim, gut and scale the fish. Preheat the oven to 180°C/350°F/Gas 4.

2 Heat the oil in a large, heavy-based saucepan and stir-fry the pine nuts for 1 minute. Add the onion and continue to stir-fry until soft but not coloured.

3 Add the chopped tomatoes and simmer for 10 minutes. Stir in the raisins, ground spices and mint, reserving a little of the spices. Add the rice and lemon. Transfer to a large roasting tin and pour over the stock.

4 Place the fish on top of the rice mixture and make several slashes in the skin with a sharp knife. Sprinkle over a little salt, and the reserved mixed spice and cinnamon.

5 Bake the fish in the preheated oven for 30–35 minutes if you are cooking a large fish and about 20–25 minutes for a smaller one. Serve immediately, garnished with some fresh sprigs of mint.

LEBANESE KIBBEH

The national dish of Syria and the Lebanon is *Kibbeh*, a kind of meatball made from minced lamb and bulgur wheat. Raw *Kibbeh* is the most widely eaten type, but this version is very popular too.

INGREDIENTS
115g/4oz/³/₄ cup bulgur wheat
450g/1lb/4 cups finely minced lean lamb
1 large onion, grated
15ml/1 tbsp melted butter
fresh mint sprigs, to garnish
rice, to serve

FOR THE FILLING
30ml/2 tbsp oil
1 onion, finely chopped
225g/8oz/2 cups minced lamb or veal
50g/2oz/¹/₂ cup pine nuts
2.5ml/¹/₂ tsp ground allspice
salt and freshly ground black pepper

FOR THE YOGURT DIP
600ml/1 pint/2¹/₂ cups Greek-style yogurt
2–3 garlic cloves, crushed
15–30ml/1–2 tbsp chopped fresh mint

SERVES 6

1 Preheat the oven to 190°C/375°F/Gas 5. Rinse the bulgur wheat in a sieve and squeeze out any excess moisture.

2 Mix the minced lamb, onion and seasoning, kneading the mixture to make a thick paste. Add the bulgur wheat and blend together.

3 To make the filling, heat the oil in a frying pan and fry the onion until golden. Add the lamb or veal and cook, stirring, until evenly browned and then add the pine nuts, allspice and salt and pepper.

4 Oil a large baking dish and spread half of the meat and bulgur wheat mixture over the bottom of it. Spoon over the filling and top it with a second layer of meat and bulgur wheat, pressing down firmly with the back of a spoon.

5 Pour the melted butter over the top of the dish and then bake in the preheated oven for about 40–45 minutes, or until it is browned on top.

6 Meanwhile, make the yogurt dip. Blend together the Greek-style yogurt and garlic and spoon it into a serving bowl. Sprinkle generously with the chopped mint.

7 Using a sharp knife, cut the cooked *Kibbeh* into squares or rectangles and serve them garnished with fresh mint and accompanied by plain boiled rice and the yogurt dip.

STUFFED TOMATOES

E ver popular, this is a recipe that demonstrates the versatility of mince, used here as a stuffing. Bulgur wheat is a good alternative to the fresh version which uses long grain rice.

INGREDIENTS
4 beef tomatoes
7.5ml/¹⁄₂ tbsp oil
75g/3oz/¹⁄₄ cup minced beef
1 small red onion, thinly sliced
25g/1oz/¹⁄₄ cup bulgur wheat
30ml/2 tbsp freshly grated
Parmesan cheese
15g/¹⁄₂oz/1 tbsp unsalted cashew
nuts, chopped
1 small celery stick, chopped
salt and freshly ground black pepper
crisp green salad, to serve

SERVES 4

1 Trim the tops from the tomatoes, scoop out the flesh with a teaspoon and reserve. Blanch the tomatoes for 2 minutes in boiling water and drain well.

2 Heat the oil in a large pan, add the beef and onion, and cook for 10 minutes. Stir in the tomato flesh. Place the bulgur wheat in a mixing bowl, cover it with boiling water and leave it to soak for 10 minutes. Drain the wheat if necessary.

3 Add the cheese, nuts and celery to the mince. Mix into the wheat and season.

4 Spoon the filling into the tomatoes. Grill under a medium heat for 10 minutes, then serve with a crisp green salad.

KOFTAS IN TOMATO SAUCE

here are many varieties of koftas in the Middle East. This is a popular version from Turkey.

INGREDIENTS
350g/12oz/3 cups minced lamb or beef
25g/1oz/¹/₂ cup fresh breadcrumbs
1 onion, grated
45ml/3 tbsp chopped fresh parsley
15ml/1 tbsp chopped fresh mint
5ml/1 tsp ground cumin
5ml/1 tsp ground turmeric
45ml/3 tbsp oil
salt and freshly ground black pepper
fresh mint leaves, to garnish
egg noodles, to serve

FOR THE TOMATO SAUCE
15ml/1 tbsp oil
1 onion, chopped
400g/14oz can plum tomatoes
15ml/1 tbsp tomato purée
juice of ¹/₂ lemon
salt and freshly ground black pepper

SERVES 4

COOK'S TIP
Instead of using minced lamb or beef, use a mixture of the two, if you like.

1 First make the tomato sauce. Heat the oil in a large saucepan or flameproof casserole and fry the onion until golden. Stir in the tomatoes, tomato purée, lemon juice and seasoning and bring to the boil. Reduce the heat and simmer the mixture for about 10 minutes.

2 Meanwhile, place the minced lamb or beef in a large bowl and mix in the breadcrumbs, grated onion, herbs and spices and a little salt and pepper.

3 Knead the mixture by hand until thoroughly blended and then shape the mixture into walnut-size meatballs and place them on a plate.

4 Heat the oil in a frying pan and fry the meatballs, in batches if necessary, until evenly browned. Transfer them to the tomato sauce. Cover the pan and simmer very gently for about 30 minutes. Serve, garnished with mint leaves, on a bed of cooked egg noodles.

MIDDLE EASTERN BEEF STEW

 ull of the added goodness of vegetables, this recipe introduces another delicious couscous dish.

INGREDIENTS
15ml/1 tbsp oil
450g/1lb/4 cups minced beef
1 garlic clove, crushed
1 onion, quartered
25g/1oz/2 tbsp plain flour
150ml/¼ pint/⅔ cup dry white wine
150ml/¼ pint/⅔ cup beef stock
2 baby turnips, chopped
115g/4oz swede, chopped
2 carrots, cut into chunks
2 courgettes, cut into chunks
15ml/1 tbsp chopped fresh coriander
5ml/1 tsp ground coriander
225g/8oz/2 cups couscous
salt and freshly ground black pepper
fresh coriander, to garnish

SERVES 4

1 Heat the oil in a frying pan. Add the beef and fry for 5 minutes. Add the garlic and onion and cook for a further 3 minutes.

2 Stir in the flour and cook for 1 minute. Add the wine and stock, season and bring to the boil, stirring all the time.

COOK'S TIP
If you are short of time, use a packaged quick-cook couscous for this recipe.

3 Add the prepared vegetables with the fresh and ground coriander. Reduce the heat, cover and cook for 15 minutes.

4 Meanwhile, place the couscous in a bowl and cover with boiling water. Leave to stand for 10 minutes. Drain and place in a lined steamer or colander. Remove the lid from the pan and place the steamer on top. Steam the couscous over the pan for a further 30 minutes. Serve with the stew, garnished with fresh coriander.

LAMB KEBABS

Skewered, grilled meats are the main item in many Middle Eastern and Greek restaurants. In this recipe, marinated lamb is grilled with a variety of fresh vegetables.

INGREDIENTS
450g/1lb boneless leg of lamb, cubed
75ml/5 tbsp olive oil
15ml/1 tbsp chopped fresh oregano or
thyme, or 10ml/2 tsp dried oregano
15ml/1 tbsp chopped fresh parsley
juice of 1/2 lemon
1/2 small aubergine, thickly sliced
and quartered
4 baby onions, halved
2 tomatoes, quartered
4 fresh bay leaves
salt and freshly ground black pepper
bulgur wheat salad, to serve

MAKES 4

COOK'S TIP
Make a lemony bulgur wheat salad to accompany the kebabs, if you like. Or serve them with plain, boiled rice – either basmati or jasmine rice would be a good choice.

1 Place the lamb in a bowl. Mix together the olive oil, oregano or thyme, parsley, lemon juice and seasoning and pour it over the lamb. Mix well. Cover the bowl and marinate for about 1 hour.

2 Preheat the grill. Thread the marinated lamb on to four large skewers, alternating with the aubergine, onions, tomatoes and bay leaves.

3 Place the kebabs on a grill rack and brush the vegetables liberally with the leftover marinade.

4 Cook the kebabs under a medium heat for about 8–10 minutes on each side, basting once or twice with the juices that have collected in the bottom of the grill pan. Serve the kebabs hot, or accompanied by the bulgur wheat salad.

TURKISH LAMB AND APRICOT STEW

I n the Middle East, meat is normally stewed or barbecued. The slightly tangy taste of dried fruit complements the richness of lamb in this satisfying casserole.

INGREDIENTS
1 large aubergine
30ml/2 tbsp sunflower oil
1 onion, chopped
1 garlic clove, crushed
5ml/1 tsp ground cinnamon
3 whole cloves
450g/1lb boned leg of lamb, cubed
400g/14oz can chopped tomatoes
115g/4oz/¹⁄₂ cup ready-to-eat dried apricots
115g/4oz canned chick-peas, drained
5ml/1 tsp clear honey
salt and freshly ground black pepper

FOR THE COUSCOUS
225g/8oz/1¹⁄₄ cups cooked couscous
30ml/2 tbsp olive oil
30ml/2 tbsp chopped almonds, fried in a little oil
chopped fresh parsley

SERVES 4

1 Cube the aubergine and place it in a colander. Sprinkle it generously with salt and allow to stand for 30 minutes.

2 Heat the sunflower oil in a flameproof casserole, add the onion and garlic and fry for 5 minutes, until softened.

3 Stir in the ground cinnamon and whole cloves and fry for about 1 minute. Add the leg of lamb and cook the mixture for about 5–6 minutes, stirring occasionally, until well browned.

4 Rinse, drain and pat dry the aubergine cubes, add them to the pan and cook for 3 minutes, stirring well. Add the tomatoes, 300ml/¹⁄₂ pint/1¹⁄₄ cups water, dried apricots and seasoning. Bring to the boil, then cover the pan with a lid and simmer gently for about 45 minutes.

5 Stir in the chick-peas and honey and cook for a further 15–20 minutes, or until the lamb is tender. Serve accompanied by couscous with the olive oil, fried almonds and chopped parsley stirred in.

LAMB COUSCOUS

ouscous can be served with all sorts of different stews. This is a popular dish from Morocco.

INGREDIENTS
45ml/3 tbsp oil
1 large onion, chopped
450g/1lb lamb, cut into 5cm/2in cubes
4 tomatoes, seeded and chopped
2 garlic cloves, halved
5ml/1 tsp ground ginger
5ml/1 tsp ground fennel seeds
5ml/1 tsp ground turmeric
2.5ml/¹/₂ tsp chilli sauce (optional)
50g/2oz/¹/₄ cup canned chick-peas
225g/8oz/1¹/₄ cups couscous
2 carrots, cut into small chunks
2 courgettes, cut into small chunks
4 new potatoes, halved
salt and freshly ground black pepper

SERVES 4

1 Heat 30ml/2 tbsp of the oil in a large saucepan and fry the chopped onion for 4–5 minutes, until softened. Add the meat and fry over a moderate heat until it is evenly browned all over.

2 Place the tomatoes, garlic, ginger, fennel seeds, turmeric and chilli sauce, if using, in a blender or food processor and process to a smooth paste.

3 Pour the tomato paste over the meat. Add the drained chick-peas and 250ml/8fl oz/1 cup water and bring to the boil. Season with salt and pepper. Reduce the heat, cover the pan and simmer gently for about 45 minutes.

4 Place the couscous in a large mixing bowl and stir in the remaining oil and about 750ml/1¼ pints/3 cups water, rubbing the couscous through your fingers to separate the grains. Set aside for about 15 minutes.

5 Add the chopped carrots, courgettes and potatoes to the stew and cook for a further 15–20 minutes.

6 Place the couscous in a steamer or colander, making several deep holes in the surface with the handle of a wooden spoon. Set over the stew, cover tightly and steam for about 10 minutes, or until the couscous is tender and no longer grainy.

7 Place the couscous on a large serving plate, make a dip in the centre and spoon over the lamb stew.

CHICKEN WITH SPICY YOGURT

Plan this dish well in advance. The extra-long marinating time is necessary to develop a really mellow spicy flavour.

INGREDIENTS
6 chicken pieces
juice of 1 lemon
5ml/1 tsp salt

FOR THE MARINADE
5ml/1 tsp coriander seeds
10ml/2 tsp cumin seeds
6 whole cloves
2 bay leaves
1 onion, quartered
2 garlic cloves
5cm/2in fresh root ginger, peeled and roughly chopped
2.5ml/¹/₂ tsp chilli powder
5ml/1 tsp turmeric
150ml/¹/₄ pint/²/₃ cup natural yogurt
lemon slices and fresh mint sprigs, to garnish
salad leaves, to serve

SERVES 6

1 Skin the chicken pieces and slash the fleshiest parts with a knife. Sprinkle over the lemon juice and salt and rub in.

2 Spread the coriander and cumin seeds, cloves and bay leaves in the bottom of a large frying pan and dry fry over a moderate heat until the bay leaves are crispy.

3 Cool the spices and grind them coarsely with a pestle and mortar.

4 Finely mince the onion, garlic and ginger in a food processor or blender. Add the ground spices, chilli powder, turmeric and yogurt, then strain in the lemon juice from the chicken.

5 Arrange the chicken pieces in a single layer in a roasting tin. Pour over the spicy marinade, then cover and chill for 24–36 hours.

6 Occasionally turn the chicken pieces in the marinade. Preheat the oven to 200°C/400°F/Gas 6. Cook the chicken for 45 minutes. Garnish with lemon and mint, and serve hot or cold with salad leaves.

CITRUS CHICKEN KEBABS

T his tangy dish makes an ideal summer lunch. Or you could serve it outside as part of a barbecue.

INGREDIENTS
4 chicken breasts, skinned and boned
fresh mint sprigs and orange, lemon or
lime slices, to garnish
salad leaves, to serve

FOR THE MARINADE
finely grated rind and juice of ¹/₂ orange
finely grated rind and juice of ¹/₂ small
lemon or lime
30ml/2 tbsp olive oil
30ml/2 tbsp clear honey
30ml/2 tbsp chopped fresh mint
1.25ml/¹/₄ tsp ground cumin
salt and freshly ground black pepper

SERVES 4

1 Cut the chicken breasts into cubes of approximately 2.5cm/1in.

2 Stir all the marinade ingredients together, with salt and pepper to taste, in a mixing bowl. Add the prepared chicken cubes and leave them to marinate for at least 2 hours.

3 Thread the chicken pieces on to skewers and grill or barbecue over low coals for 15 minutes, basting with the marinade and turning frequently. Garnish with mint and citrus slices and serve with salad leaves.

DUCK BREASTS WITH A WALNUT
AND POMEGRANATE SAUCE

 his is an extremely exotic sweet and sour dish which originally came from Persia.

INGREDIENTS
60ml/4 tbsp olive oil
2 onions, very thinly sliced
2.5ml/¹/₂ tsp ground turmeric
400g/14oz/3¹/₂ cups walnuts,
roughly chopped
1 litre/1³/₄ pints/4 cups duck or
chicken stock
6 pomegranates
30ml/2 tbsp caster sugar
60ml/4 tbsp lemon juice
4 duck breasts, about 225g/8oz each
salt and freshly ground black pepper

SERVES 4

1 Heat half the oil in a frying pan, add the onions and turmeric, and cook until soft. Transfer to a saucepan, add the walnuts and stock, then season. Stir, bring to the boil and simmer, uncovered, for 20 minutes.

2 Cut the pomegranates in half and scoop out the seeds. Reserve the seeds of one pomegranate. Transfer the remaining seeds to a blender or food processor and process. Strain through a sieve, to extract the juice, and stir in the sugar and lemon juice.

COOK'S TIP
Choose pomegranates with shiny, brightly coloured skins. The juice stains, so take care when cutting them. Only the seeds are used in cooking, the pith is discarded.

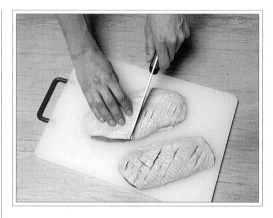

3 Score the skin of the duck breasts in a lattice fashion with a knife. Heat the remaining oil in a frying pan or chargrill and place the duck breasts in it, skin side down.

4 Cook gently for 10 minutes, pouring off the fat from time to time, until the skin is dark golden and crisp. Turn them over and cook for a further 3–4 minutes. Transfer to a plate and leave to rest.

5 Deglaze the frying pan or chargrill with the pomegranate juice mixture, stirring with a wooden spoon, then add the walnut and stock mixture and simmer for about 15 minutes, or until the sauce has thickened slightly. Serve the duck breasts sliced, drizzled with a little sauce, and garnished with the reserved pomegranate seeds. Serve the remaining sauce separately.

CHICKEN COUSCOUS

 ouscous is a form of semolina, and is a delicious accompaniment or stuffing for many dishes.

INGREDIENTS
15ml/1 tbsp butter
15ml/1 tbsp sunflower oil
4 chicken portions
2 onions, finely chopped
2 garlic cloves, crushed
2.5ml/¹/₂ tsp ground cinnamon
1.25ml/¹/₄ tsp ground ginger
1.25ml/¹/₄ tsp ground turmeric
30ml/2 tbsp orange juice
10ml/2 tsp clear honey
salt and freshly ground black pepper
fresh mint sprigs, to garnish

FOR THE COUSCOUS
350g/12oz/2¹/₄ cups couscous
5ml/1 tsp salt
10ml/2 tsp caster sugar
30ml/2 tbsp sunflower oil
2.5ml/¹/₂ tsp ground cinnamon
pinch of grated nutmeg
15ml/1 tbsp orange flower water
30ml/2 tbsp sultanas
50g/2oz/¹/₂ cup blanched almonds
45ml/3 tbsp chopped pistachio nuts

SERVES 4

1 Heat the butter and oil in a large pan and add the chicken portions, skin side down. Fry for 3–4 minutes, until the skin is golden, then turn over.

2 Add the onions, garlic, spices and a pinch of salt and pour over the orange juice and 300ml/½ pint/1¼ cups water. Cover and bring to the boil, then reduce the heat and simmer for about 30 minutes.

3 Place the couscous and salt in a bowl and cover with 350ml/12fl oz/1½ cups water. Stir once and leave to stand for about 5 minutes. Add the caster sugar, 15ml/1 tbsp of the oil, the cinnamon, nutmeg, orange flower water and sultanas to the couscous and mix well.

4 Chop the almonds, heat the remaining oil in a pan and lightly fry them until golden. Stir into the couscous with the pistachio nuts.

5 Line a steamer with greaseproof paper and spoon in the couscous. Sit the steamer over the chicken (or over a pan of boiling water) and steam for 10 minutes.

6 Remove the steamer from the heat and keep covered. Stir the honey into the chicken liquid and boil it rapidly for about 3–4 minutes. Spoon the couscous on to a warmed serving platter and place the chicken on top, with a little of the sauce spooned over. Garnish with fresh mint and serve with the remaining sauce.

CHICKEN WITH LEMONS AND OLIVES

Lemons and olives create a gentle flavour that enhances all kinds of meat and fish dishes, such as this.

INGREDIENTS

2.5ml/¹/₂ tsp ground cinnamon
2.5ml/¹/₂ tsp ground turmeric
1.5kg/3–3¹/₂lb chicken
30ml/2 tbsp olive oil
1 large onion, thinly sliced
5cm/2in fresh root ginger, grated
600ml/1 pint/2¹/₂ cups chicken stock
2 preserved lemons or limes, or fresh ones, cut into wedges
75g/3oz/¹/₂ cup brown olives, stoned
15ml/1 tbsp clear honey
60ml/4 tbsp chopped fresh coriander
salt and freshly ground black pepper
fresh coriander sprigs, to garnish

SERVES 4

1 Preheat the oven to 190°C/375°F/Gas 5. Mix the ground cinnamon and turmeric in a bowl with a little salt and pepper and rub it all over the chicken skin to give an even coating.

2 Heat the oil in a large sauté or shallow frying pan and fry the chicken on all sides until it turns golden. Transfer the chicken to an ovenproof dish.

3 Add the sliced onion to the pan and fry for 3 minutes. Stir in the grated ginger and the chicken stock and bring it just to the boil. Pour over the chicken, cover with a lid and bake in the oven for 30 minutes.

4 Remove the chicken from the oven and add the lemons or limes, brown olives and honey.

5 Bake the dish, uncovered, for a further 45 minutes until the chicken is tender.

6 Stir in the fresh coriander and season to taste. Garnish with coriander sprigs and serve at once.

CHICKEN FILO PIE

This is based on a Greek chicken pie, called *Kotopitta*. You could substitute the feta with some chopped dried apricots for a more fruity alternative, if you like.

INGREDIENTS
275g/10oz filo pastry
30ml/2 tbsp olive oil
75g/3oz/¹⁄₂ cup chopped toasted almonds
30ml/2 tbsp milk
fresh mint sprigs, to garnish
salad, to serve

FOR THE FILLING
15ml/1 tbsp olive oil
1 onion, finely chopped
1 garlic clove, crushed
450g/1lb boned and cooked chicken
50g/2oz feta cheese, crumbled
15ml/1 tbsp chopped fresh parsley
15ml/1 tbsp chopped fresh coriander
15ml/1 tbsp chopped fresh mint
2 eggs, beaten
salt and freshly ground black pepper

SERVES 4

1 For the filling, heat the olive oil in a large frying pan and cook the onion gently until tender. Add the garlic clove and cook for a further 2 minutes, then transfer to a mixing bowl.

2 Remove the skin from the cooked chicken and mince or chop it finely with a sharp knife. Add it to the onion in the bowl, along with the feta cheese, fresh herbs and beaten eggs. Mix everything together thoroughly and season with salt and freshly ground black pepper.

3 Preheat the oven to 190°C/375°F/Gas 5. Have a damp dish cloth close to hand to keep the filo pastry covered at all times. You will need to work fast with filo pastry, as it dries out very quickly once it is exposed to the air. Unravel the filo pastry from the packet and cut the whole batch into a 30cm/12in square.

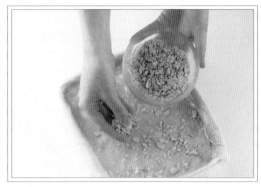

4 Taking half the sheets (cover the remainder with the dish cloth), brush one sheet with olive oil, lay it on a greased 1.5 litre/2½ pint/6¼ cups ovenproof dish and sprinkle with a few chopped toasted almonds. Repeat with the other filo sheets, overlapping them alternately in the dish.

5 Spoon in the filling and cover the pie in the same way with the rest of the overlapping pastry.

6 Fold in the overlapping edges and mark a diamond pattern on the surface of the pie with a sharp knife.

7 Brush with milk and sprinkle on any remaining almonds. Bake the pie for 20–30 minutes, or until it is golden brown on top. Remove from the oven, garnish with mint, and serve with a salad.

TABBOULEH WITH FENNEL AND POMEGRANATE

This fresh salad, originating in the Middle East, has the added crunchiness of fennel and sweet pomegranate seeds. It is perfect for a summer lunch. Try and make it the day before as this improves the flavour.

INGREDIENTS
225g/8oz/1 cup bulgur wheat
2 fennel bulbs
1 small fresh red chilli, seeded and finely chopped
1 celery stick, finely sliced
30ml/2 tbsp olive oil
finely grated rind and juice of 2 lemons
6–8 spring onions, chopped
90ml/6 tbsp chopped fresh mint
90ml/6 tbsp chopped fresh parsley
1 pomegranate, seeds removed
salt and freshly ground black pepper
salad leaves, to serve

SERVES 6

VARIATION
You can add a variety of ingredients to this delicious dish. Instead of fennel and pomegranate, try adding chopped tomatoes, peppers and olives.

1 Place the bulgur wheat in a bowl and pour over enough cold water to cover. Leave to stand for 30 minutes.

2 Carefully drain the bulgur wheat through a sieve, pressing out any excess water with a spoon.

3 Halve the fennel bulbs and cut them into very fine slices.

4 Mix all the remaining ingredients together, including the soaked bulgur wheat and fennel. Season well, cover, and set aside for 30 minutes before serving with salad leaves.

SWEET VEGETABLE COUSCOUS

A wonderful combination of sweet vegetables and spices, this makes a substantial winter dish.

INGREDIENTS
generous pinch of saffron threads
15ml/1 tbsp olive oil
1 red onion, sliced
2 garlic cloves
1–2 fresh red chillies, seeded and finely chopped
2.5ml/¹/₂ tsp ground ginger
2.5ml/¹/₂ tsp ground cinnamon
400g/14oz can chopped tomatoes
300ml/¹/₂ pint/1¹/₄ cups vegetable stock or water
4 carrots, peeled and cut into 5mm/¹/₄in slices
2 turnips, peeled and cut into 2cm/³/₄in cubes
450g/1lb sweet potatoes, peeled and cut into 2cm/³/₄in cubes
75g/3oz/²/₃ cup raisins
2 courgettes, cut into 5mm/¹/₄in slices
400g/14oz can chick-peas, drained and rinsed
45ml/3 tbsp chopped fresh parsley
45ml/3 tbsp chopped fresh coriander
450g/1lb quick-cook couscous

SERVES 4–6

1 Leave the saffron to infuse in 45ml/3 tbsp boiling water.

2 Heat the oil in a large saucepan. Add the onion, garlic and chillies and cook gently for 5 minutes.

3 Add the ground ginger and cinnamon and cook for a further 1–2 minutes.

4 Add the tomatoes, stock or water, infused saffron and liquid, carrots, turnips, sweet potatoes and raisins, cover and simmer for 25 minutes.

5 Add the courgettes, drained chick-peas, parsley and coriander and cook for another 10 minutes.

6 Meanwhile, prepare the quick-cook couscous following the packet instructions and serve it immediately with the sweet vegetables.

PERSIAN RICE AND LENTILS WITH A TAHDEEG

Persian or Iranian cuisine is an exotic and delicious one, steeped in history. Flavours are intense and somehow more sophisticated than other Middle Eastern styles. *Tahdeeg* is the glorious, golden rice crust that forms at the bottom of the saucepan.

INGREDIENTS

450g/1lb/2³/₄ cups basmati rice, rinsed thoroughly and soaked
2 onions, 1 chopped and 1 thinly sliced
2 garlic cloves, crushed
150ml/¹/₄ pint/²/₃ cup sunflower oil
50g/2oz/1 cup green lentils, soaked
600ml/1 pint/2¹/₂ cups vegetable stock
50g/2oz/¹/₃ cup raisins
45ml/3 tbsp tomato purée
10ml/2 tsp ground coriander
few strands of saffron
1 egg yolk, beaten
10ml/2 tsp natural yogurt
75g/3oz/6 tbsp butter, melted and strained
oil, for frying
salt and freshly ground black pepper
flat leaf parsley, to garnish

SERVES 8

1 Boil the rinsed and drained rice in plenty of well-salted water for 3 minutes only. Drain again.

2 Meanwhile, fry the chopped onion and garlic in 30ml/2 tbsp of oil for 5 minutes then add the lentils, stock, raisins, tomato purée, coriander and seasoning. Bring to the boil, then cover and simmer for 20 minutes. Set aside.

3 Soak the saffron in a little hot water. Remove about 120ml/8 tbsp of the rice and mix with the egg yolk and yogurt. Season well.

4 In a large pan, heat about two-thirds of the remaining oil and scatter the egg and yogurt rice evenly over the base.

5 Scatter the remaining rice into the pan, alternating it with the lentils. Build up in a pyramid shape away from the sides of the pan, finishing with plain rice on top.

6 With a long wooden spoon handle, make three holes down to the bottom of the pan and drizzle over the butter. Bring to a high heat, then wrap the pan lid in a clean, wet dish cloth and place on top. When a good head of steam appears, turn the heat down to low. Cook for about 30 minutes.

7 Meanwhile, fry the sliced onion in the remaining oil until browned and crisp. Drain well and set aside.

8 Remove the rice pan from the heat, still covered, and stand it briefly in a sink of cold water for 1–2 minutes to loosen the base. Remove the lid and mix a few spoons of the white rice with the saffron water.

9 Toss the rice and lentils together in the pan and spoon out on to a serving dish in a mound. Scatter the saffron rice on top. Break up the rice crust on the bottom (the prized *tahdeeg*) and place it around the mound. Scatter the fried onion on top of the saffron rice and serve it garnished with flat leaf parsley.

CHICK-PEA FALAFEL WITH CORIANDER DIP

Little balls of spicy chick-pea purée, deep fried until crisp, are served with a coriander-flavoured mayonnaise. Falafel are a typical street food in Israel, where they are served hot and crisp in warm pitta bread.

INGREDIENTS
400g/14oz can chick-peas, drained
6 spring onions, sliced
1 egg
2.5ml/¹/₂ tsp ground turmeric
1 garlic clove, crushed
5ml/1 tsp ground cumin
60ml/4 tbsp chopped fresh coriander
oil, for deep frying
1 small red chilli, seeded and
finely chopped
45ml/3 tbsp mayonnaise
salt and freshly ground black pepper
fresh coriander sprig, to garnish

SERVES 4

1 Tip the chick-peas into a food processor or blender. Add the spring onions and process to a smooth paste. Add the egg, turmeric, garlic, cumin and 15ml/1 tbsp of the chopped coriander. Process briefly to mix, then add salt and pepper to taste.

2 Working with clean wet hands, shape the processed chick-pea mixture into about 16 balls.

3 Heat the oil for deep frying to a temperature of 180°C/350°F, or until a cube of bread added to the oil browns in 30–45 seconds. Deep fry the falafel, in batches, for 2–3 minutes or until they turn golden. Drain them well on kitchen paper, then place in a serving bowl.

4 Stir the remaining coriander and the chopped chilli into the mayonnaise and place in a small bowl, garnished with a coriander sprig. Serve the falafel, hot or cold, with the coriander dip.

PITTAS STUFFED WITH SALAD

The Greek name for this classic salad is *Horiatiki*. It is made with feta, a cheese made from ewes' milk. Try serving it in hot pitta breads with a minty yogurt dressing.

INGREDIENTS

115g/4oz/1 cup diced feta cheese
¼ cucumber, peeled and diced
8 cherry tomatoes, quartered
½ small green pepper, seeded and thinly sliced
¼ small onion, thinly sliced
8 black olives, stoned and halved
30ml/2 tbsp olive oil
5ml/1 tsp dried oregano
4 large pitta breads
60ml/4 tbsp Greek-style yogurt
5ml/1 tsp dried mint
salt and freshly ground black pepper
fresh mint, to garnish

MAKES 4

1 Place the feta cheese, diced cucumber, cherry tomatoes, green pepper, onion and black olives in a mixing bowl. Stir in the olive oil and oregano, then season well and set aside.

2 Place the pitta breads in a toaster or under a grill for about 2 minutes, until puffed up. Meanwhile, mix the yogurt with the mint, season well and reserve.

3 Holding the hot pittas in a dish cloth, slice each one from top to bottom down one of the longest sides and open out to form a pocket.

4 Divide the prepared salad among the pitta breads and drizzle over a spoonful of the dressing. Serve the pittas at once, garnished with fresh mint.

IMAM BAYILDI

Legend has it that a Muslim holy man – the Imam – was so overwhelmed by this dish that he fainted in sheer delight! Translated, *Imam Bayildi* means "the Imam fainted".

INGREDIENTS

2 aubergines, seeded and halved
lengthways
60ml/4 tbsp olive oil
2 large onions, sliced thinly
2 garlic cloves, crushed
1 green pepper, seeded and sliced
400g/14oz can chopped tomatoes
40g/1¹/₂oz sugar
5ml/1 tsp ground coriander
salt and freshly ground black pepper
30ml/2 tbsp chopped fresh coriander or
parsley, plus extra to garnish
crusty bread, to serve

SERVES 4

COOK'S TIP
To prepare aubergines, sprinkle cut slices with salt and allow the juices that form to drain away in a colander. After 30 minutes or so, rinse well and pat dry. Aubergines prepared like this are less bitter and easier to cook.

---

1 Using a sharp knife, slash the flesh of the aubergines a few times. Sprinkle with salt and place in a colander for about 30 minutes. Rinse well and pat dry.

2 Gently fry the aubergines, cut side down, in the oil for 5 minutes, then drain and place in a shallow ovenproof dish.

3 In the same pan, gently fry the onions, garlic and green pepper, adding extra oil if necessary. Cook for about 10 minutes, until the vegetables have softened.

4 Preheat the oven to 190°C/375°F/Gas 5. Add the tomatoes, sugar, ground coriander and seasoning to the pan and cook for about 5 minutes until the mixture is reduced. Stir in the chopped herbs.

5 Spoon the tomato mixture on top of the aubergines in the dish, cover and bake for 30–35 minutes. When cooked, cool, then chill. Garnish with coriander or parsley and serve cold with plenty of crusty bread.

FATTOUSH

T his simple peasant salad has become a popular dish all over Syria and the Lebanon. You can add as many fresh herbs as you like.

INGREDIENTS
1 yellow or red pepper
1 large cucumber
4–5 tomatoes
1 bunch spring onions
30ml/2 tbsp finely chopped fresh parsley
30ml/2 tbsp finely chopped fresh mint
30ml/2 tbsp finely chopped fresh coriander
2 garlic cloves, crushed
75ml/5 tbsp olive oil
juice of 2 lemons
salt and freshly ground black pepper
2 pitta breads

SERVES 4

COOK'S TIP
If you prefer, make this salad in the traditional way. After toasting the pitta bread until crisp, crush it in your hand and then sprinkle it over the salad before serving.

1 Slice the pepper, discarding the seeds and core, then roughly chop the cucumber and tomatoes. Place them in a large salad bowl.

2 Trim and slice the spring onions. Add them to the cucumber, tomatoes and pepper, along with the finely chopped parsley, mint and coriander.

3 To make the dressing, blend the garlic with the olive oil and lemon juice in a jug, then season to taste with salt and black pepper. Pour the dressing over the salad and toss lightly to mix.

4 Toast the pitta bread in a toaster or under a hot grill until crisp and then serve it with the salad.

OKRA WITH CORIANDER AND TOMATOES

kra is a delicious vegetable. It releases a sticky sap when cooked, which helps to thicken the dish.

INGREDIENTS
450g/1lb fresh tomatoes, or 400g/14oz
can chopped tomatoes
450g/1lb fresh okra
45ml/3 tbsp olive oil
2 onions, thinly sliced
10ml/2 tsp coriander seeds, crushed
3 garlic cloves, crushed
2.5ml/¹/₂ tsp caster sugar
freshly grated rind and juice of 1 lemon
salt and freshly ground black pepper

SERVES 4

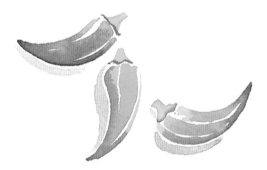

1 If using fresh tomatoes, plunge them into boiling water for 30 seconds, then refresh in cold water and peel away the skins. Chop roughly.

2 Trim off any stalks from the fresh okra and leave them whole. Heat the olive oil in a sauté pan and fry the onions and coriander seeds for 3–4 minutes until they start to colour.

3 Add the okra and garlic and fry for 1 minute. Gently stir in the tomatoes and sugar and simmer gently for 20 minutes, or until the okra is tender, stirring once or twice. Stir in the lemon rind and juice and add salt and pepper to taste, adding a little more sugar, if necessary. Serve the dish warm or cold.

COOK'S TIP
Buy okra only if it is soft and velvety, not if it is dry and shrivelled.

SEMOLINA AND NUT HALVA

Semolina is a popular ingredient in many desserts and pastries in the Middle East. Here, it provides a spongy base for soaking up a deliciously fragrant spicy syrup.

INGREDIENTS
115g/4oz/¹/₂ cup unsalted butter, softened
115g/4oz/¹/₂ cup caster sugar
finely grated rind of 1 orange, plus
30ml/2 tbsp juice
3 eggs
175g/6oz/1 cup semolina
10ml/2 tsp baking powder
115g/4oz/1 cup ground hazelnuts

FOR THE SYRUP
350g/12oz/1¹/₂ cups caster sugar
2 cinnamon sticks, halved
juice of 1 lemon
60ml/4 tbsp orange flower water
50g/2oz/¹/₂ cup unblanched hazelnuts,
toasted and chopped
50g/2oz/¹/₂ cup blanched almonds,
toasted and chopped
shredded rind of 1 orange

SERVES 10

1 Preheat the oven to 220°C/425°F/Gas 7. Grease and line the base of a deep 23cm/9in square solid-based cake tin.

2 Lightly cream the butter in a mixing bowl. Add the sugar, orange rind and juice, eggs, semolina, baking powder and hazelnuts and beat the ingredients together until smooth.

3 Turn into the prepared tin and level the surface. Bake for 20–25 minutes, until just firm and golden. Leave to cool in the tin.

4 To make the syrup, put the sugar in a small heavy-based saucepan with 575ml/18fl oz/2¼ cups water and the halved cinnamon sticks. Heat gently, stirring, until the sugar has dissolved completely.

5 Boil fast, without stirring, for 5 minutes. Add the lemon juice and flower water to half the syrup and pour it over the halva. Leave the rest of the syrup in the pan.

6 Leave the halva in the tin until the syrup is absorbed, then turn it out on to a plate and cut it diagonally into diamond-shaped portions. Scatter with the nuts.

7 Boil the remaining syrup until slightly thickened, then pour it over the halva. Scatter the orange rind over the cake.

COOK'S TIP
Halva is delicious when served with lightly whipped or clotted cream.

OMM ALI

This Egyptian version of bread and butter pudding is made with pistachio nuts and filo pastry – a truly delicious dessert.

INGREDIENTS
10–12 sheets filo pastry
600ml/1 pint/2½ cups milk
250ml/8fl oz/1 cup double cream
1 egg, beaten
30ml/2 tbsp rose water
50g/2oz/½ cup each chopped pistachio nuts, almonds and hazelnuts
115g/4oz/¾ cup raisins
15ml/1 tbsp ground cinnamon
single cream, to serve

SERVES 4

1 Preheat the oven to 160°C/325°F/Gas 3. Bake the filo pastry, on a baking sheet, for 15–20 minutes until crisp. Remove from the oven and raise the temperature to 200°C/400°F/Gas 6.

2 Scald the milk and cream by pouring them into a pan and heating very gently until hot, but not boiling. Slowly add the beaten egg and the rose water. Cook over a very low heat, until the mixture begins to thicken, stirring all the time.

3 Crumble the pastry using your hands and spread it in layers with the pistachio nuts, almonds, hazelnuts and raisins over the base of a shallow baking dish.

4 Pour the custard mixture over the nut and pastry base and bake in the oven for 20 minutes, until golden. Sprinkle with cinnamon and serve with single cream.

FRESH FIG, APPLE AND DATE SALAD

Sweet figs and dates combine especially well with crisp dessert apples. Use fresh figs if you can find them. A hint of almond serves to unite the flavours.

INGREDIENTS
6 large apples
juice of ½ lemon
175g/6oz fresh dates
25g/1oz white marzipan
5ml/1 tsp orange flower water
60ml/4 tbsp natural yogurt
4 green or purple figs
4 toasted almonds, to decorate

SERVES 4

1 Core the apples. Slice thinly, then cut them into fine matchsticks. Moisten with lemon juice to keep them white.

2 Remove the stones from the dates and cut the flesh into fine strips, then combine them with the apple slices.

3 Soften the white marzipan with orange flower water and combine it with the yogurt. Mix well.

4 Pile the apples and dates in the centre of four plates. Remove the stem from each of the figs and divide the fruit into quarters, without cutting right through the base. Squeeze the base with the thumb and forefinger of each hand to open up the fruit.

5 Place a fig in the centre of the salad, spoon in the yogurt filling and decorate with a toasted almond.

DATE-FILLED PASTRIES

From Gibraltar to Baghdad, people would get together to make hundreds of these labour-intensive pastries or *Ma-amoul*, as they are called.

INGREDIENTS
75g/3oz/6 tbsp margarine or butter, softened
175g/6oz/1½ cups plain flour
5ml/1 tsp rose water
5ml/1 tsp orange flower water
20ml/4 tsp sifted icing sugar, for sprinkling

FOR THE FILLING
115g/4oz/³⁄₄ cup stoned dried dates
2.5ml/½ tsp orange flower water

MAKES ABOUT 25

COOK'S TIP
The secret of good *Ma-amoul* is to get as much date filling into the pastry as possible, but you must make sure to seal the opening well. Traditionally, they were decorated with tweezers, but it is quicker to use a fork.

1 To make the filling, chop the dates finely. Add 50ml/2fl oz/¼ cup boiling water and the orange flower water, beat the mixture vigorously and leave to cool.

2 To make the pastries, rub the margarine or butter into the flour. Add the rose and orange flower waters and 45ml/3 tbsp water and mix to a firm dough.

3 Using your hands, shape the pastry dough into about 25 small balls.

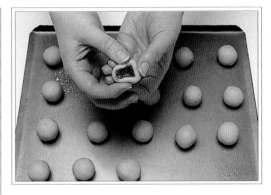

4 Preheat the oven to 180°C/350°F/Gas 4. Press your finger into each ball to make a small container, pressing the sides round and round to make the walls thinner. Put 1.5ml/¼ tsp of the date mixture into each one and seal by pressing the pastry together.

5 Arrange the date pastries, seam side down, on a lightly greased baking sheet and prick each one with a fork. Bake for 15–20 minutes and cool.

6 Put the cooled pastries on a plate and sprinkle over the icing sugar. Shake lightly to make sure they are covered.

COOK'S TIP
Ma-amoul freeze well, so make a large batch to keep in stock.

BAKLAVA

Sweet syrup-soaked pastries are popular in Greece and the Middle East. This version is flavoured with lemon and rose water.

INGREDIENTS
200g/7oz/1 cup shelled pistachio nuts
5ml/1 tsp caster sugar
10ml/2 tsp rose water
275g/10oz filo pastry
50ml/2fl oz/¼ cup oil

FOR THE SYRUP
300g/11oz/1½ cups caster sugar
juice of 1 lemon

MAKES ABOUT 30

1 Chop the pistachio nuts in a food processor or blender. Don't grind them too finely. Stir in the sugar and rose water.

2 Preheat the oven to 180°C/350°F/Gas 4. Cut the sheets of filo pastry in half. Brush a little oil on to the base and sides of a 25cm/10in square baking tin. Put in a sheet of pastry, brush with oil and cover with a second sheet. Use up half of the pastry in this way.

3 Spread the nut mixture over the pastry and cover with a filo sheet. Repeat until the oil and pastry are used up.

4 Using a sharp knife, cut vertical lines 4cm/1⅛in apart. Cut right through the pastry and nuts, then cut diagonal lines to form diamond shapes. Bake in the centre of the oven for 15–20 minutes.

5 For the syrup, put 175ml/6fl oz/¾ cup water with the sugar in a small pan and heat slowly. Stir once or twice. When it boils, add 30ml/2 tbsp lemon juice and boil for 6 minutes. Stir in the remaining lemon juice and leave to cool and thicken slightly.

6 After 20 minutes turn the oven temperature to 150°C/300°F/Gas 2 and cook the baklava for another 20 minutes. Cool for about 10 minutes.

7 Pour the syrup over the baklava. Leave for several hours or overnight so that the syrup is absorbed, and serve.

SWEET PUDDING

his is a popular pudding in Arab countries. It has a smooth silky texture and a subtle flavour.

INGREDIENTS
50g/2oz/¼ cup ground rice
45ml/3 tbsp cornflour
1.2 litres/2 pints/5 cups milk
75g/3oz/6 tbsp sugar
30ml/2 tbsp rose water
50g/2oz/½ cup ground almonds
25g/1oz/¼ cup ground pistachio nuts
ground cinnamon, to decorate

SERVES 4

1 Blend the ground rice and cornflour to a paste with a little cold milk in a small mixing bowl.

2 Bring the remaining milk to the boil, add the sugar and simmer gently. Gradually add the ground rice paste to the milk, stirring it constantly with a wooden spoon to mix.

3 Simmer the mixture on a very gentle heat for 10–15 minutes, until the mixture has thickened, stirring frequently and being very careful not to burn the bottom of the pan, which would damage the delicate flavour of the rice.

4 Stir in the rose water and half the almonds. Simmer for 5 minutes.

5 Cool for a few minutes, then pour into a bowl. Sprinkle with the remaining almonds and the pistachio nuts. Decorate with a dusting of ground cinnamon.

COOK'S TIP
Sweet Pudding is delicious when served with melted syrup or honey.

INDEX